DONOVAN BIXLEY'S

Draw Some Awesome

DRAWING TIPS & IDEAS FOR BUDDING ARTISTS

First published in Great Britain in 2023
Search Press Limited
Wellwood, North Farm Road,
Tunbridge Wells, Kent TN2 3DR

Illustrations and text copyright © Donovan Bixley, 2023
First published by Upstart Press Ltd, Auckland,
New Zealand, 2021
Published in agreement with Upstart Press Ltd

ISBN: 978-1-80092-132-0
ebook ISBN: 978-1-80093-122-0
The Publishers and author can accept no responsibility for any consequences arising from the information, advice or instructions given in this publication.

Suppliers
If you have difficulty in obtaining any of the materials and equipment mentioned in this book, then please visit the Search Press website for details of suppliers:
www.searchpress.com

You are invited to visit the author's website:
www.donovanbixley.com

SEARCH PRESS

MIX
Paper | Supporting responsible forestry
FSC® C016973

Hey Bixley, draw me a truck, or else!

Hmmm ... no wonder I don't like drawing trucks.

NOW I'M ALL GROWN UP AND I MAKE MY LIVING WRITING STORIES AND DRAWING PICTURES. I'VE WORKED ON A WHOLE PILE OF BOOKS.

I've also created illustrations for magazines, products and murals, and I've worked as a character designer on animated TV shows.

BUT I DON'T WANT YOU TO DRAW LIKE ME. I WANT TO TEACH YOU HOW TO DRAW LIKE *YOU!*

THIS BOOK IS FULL OF COOL TIPS AND IDEAS TO USE ON YOUR OWN ORIGINAL DRAWINGS.

3

WHEN I WAS A BOY, I STARTED OFF BY MAKING MY OWN BOOKS.

I would draw on any paper I could find around the house, then staple the pages together.

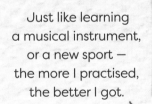

My books got bigger and my drawings got more detailed.

ALONG THE WAY I DISCOVERED FAMOUS ARTISTS THAT I LIKED.

These artists still give me lots of inspiration even though they lived many centuries ago.

Just like learning a musical instrument, or a new sport — the more I practised, the better I got.

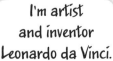

I'm artist and inventor Leonardo da Vinci.

Pronounced 'da Vin-chee'.

I'm musical genius Wolfgang Mozart. I don't know much about drawing, but I DO know about being a creative child.

Pronounced 'Mote-zart'.

I'm painter Edgar Degas.

Pronounced 'Day-gar'.

DRAWING IS JUST DREAMING WITH A PENCIL IN YOUR HAND.

As I grew older, I discovered that drawing is the basic starting point for lots of creative people.

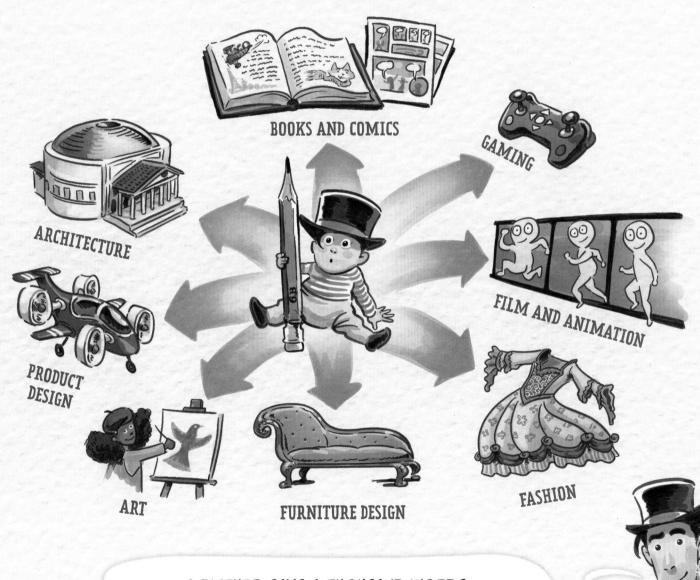

BOOKS AND COMICS

GAMING

ARCHITECTURE

FILM AND ANIMATION

PRODUCT DESIGN

ART

FURNITURE DESIGN

FASHION

A PICTURE SAYS A THOUSAND WORDS.
IF YOU CAN DRAW, YOU CAN COMMUNICATE YOUR IDEAS WITH IMAGES INSTEAD OF WORDS.

SO LET'S GRAB A PENCIL AND
PAPER AND GET DRAWING!

WARM-UP EXERCISES

Drawing is all about
getting your eye and hand
to work together.
Like sport, the more you
practise, the better you get.

TRY THIS EXERCISE
Try to draw a perfect circle in one
stroke. Draw it fast, draw it slow,
draw it big, draw it small.

I feel like I'm
going around
in circles!

URRGH! IT'S HARD TO DRAW
SOMETHING PERFECT THE FIRST TIME,
EVEN IF YOU'RE A REALLY GOOD ARTIST.

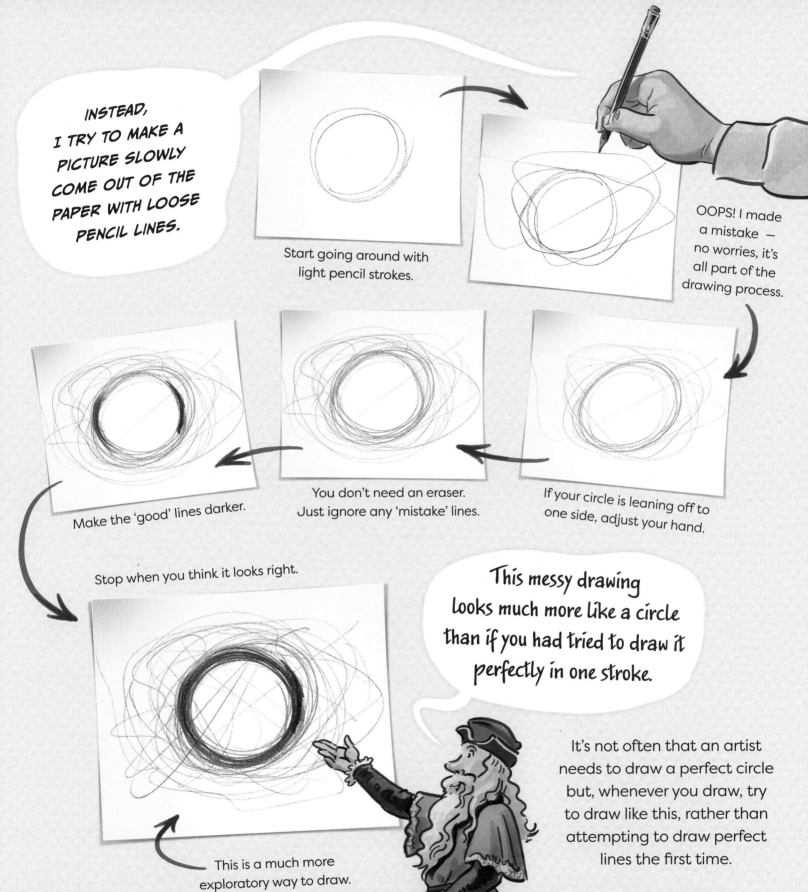

INSTEAD, I TRY TO MAKE A PICTURE SLOWLY COME OUT OF THE PAPER WITH LOOSE PENCIL LINES.

Start going around with light pencil strokes.

OOPS! I made a mistake — no worries, it's all part of the drawing process.

Make the 'good' lines darker.

You don't need an eraser. Just ignore any 'mistake' lines.

If your circle is leaning off to one side, adjust your hand.

Stop when you think it looks right.

This messy drawing looks much more like a circle than if you had tried to draw it perfectly in one stroke.

This is a much more exploratory way to draw.

It's not often that an artist needs to draw a perfect circle but, whenever you draw, try to draw like this, rather than attempting to draw perfect lines the first time.

HOW I DRAW
SIMPLE ANIMALS

Basic shapes like these are a good starting point for drawing.

DRAWING IS A BIT LIKE MAGIC. YOU START WITH A BLANK PIECE OF PAPER AND THEN THE ARTIST MAKES SOMETHING APPEAR ON IT.

IT'S ALSO LIKE A TRICK BECAUSE ALL DRAWINGS ARE MADE UP OF SIMPLE SHAPES.

I love drawing animals.

Let's see if we can draw a fantail using only simple shapes and lines.

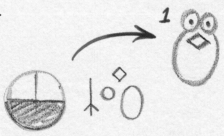

1 To draw a penguin, I start with a long pear shape.

2 Add circle eyes and a diamond-shaped beak.

3 Use triangles for flippers and feet.

4 Round out the sharp corners to make the penguin softer.

8

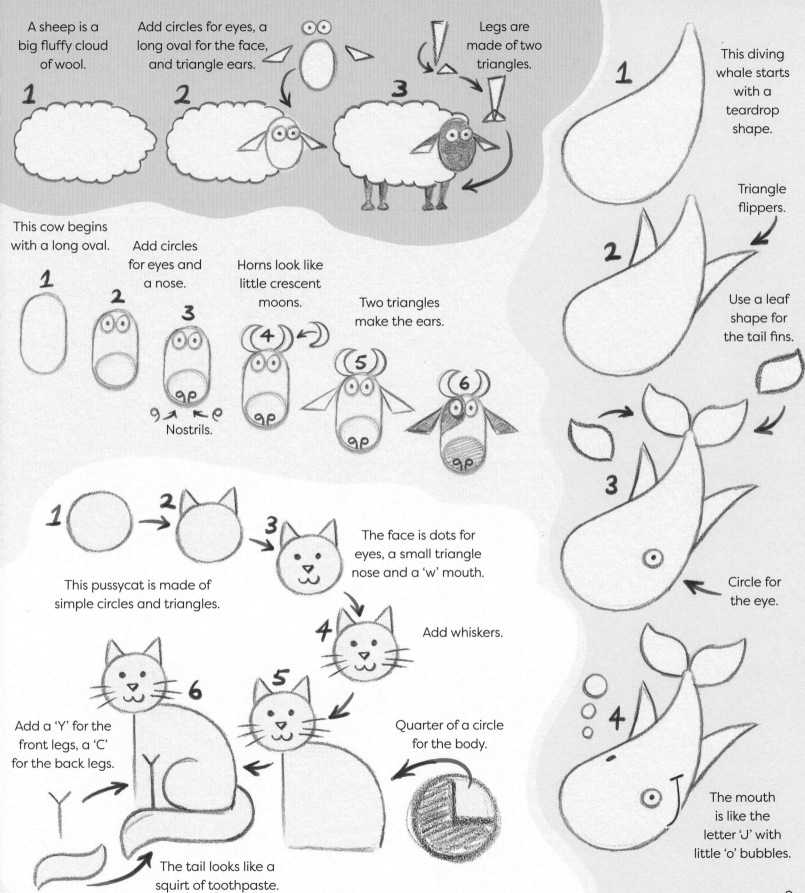

A sheep is a big fluffy cloud of wool.

1

Add circles for eyes, a long oval for the face, and triangle ears.

2

Legs are made of two triangles.

3

This cow begins with a long oval.

1

Add circles for eyes and a nose.

2

3

Nostrils.

Horns look like little crescent moons.

4

Two triangles make the ears.

5

6

This pussycat is made of simple circles and triangles.

1 **2** **3**

The face is dots for eyes, a small triangle nose and a 'w' mouth.

4

Add whiskers.

5

Quarter of a circle for the body.

6

Add a 'Y' for the front legs, a 'C' for the back legs.

The tail looks like a squirt of toothpaste.

This diving whale starts with a teardrop shape.

1

Triangle flippers.

2

Use a leaf shape for the tail fins.

3

Circle for the eye.

4

The mouth is like the letter 'J' with little 'o' bubbles.

MARK MAKING

YOU DON'T HAVE TO HAVE A WHOLE BUNCH OF FANCY DRAWING EQUIPMENT.

LIKE LEONARDO, YOU CAN COME UP WITH THE GREATEST DESIGNS WITH JUST A PIECE OF PAPER AND A PENCIL.

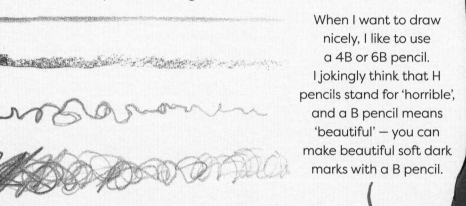

Try these different ways of drawing.

Smooth

Rough

Spidery

Scribbly

Cross-hatch

Dotty

Blended

When I want to draw nicely, I like to use a 4B or 6B pencil. I jokingly think that H pencils stand for 'horrible', and a B pencil means 'beautiful' — you can make beautiful soft dark marks with a B pencil.

When I'm sketching for a book I usually draw on a Zeta pad, which has nice smooth paper and is also good for tracing.

This is a drawing I did on a napkin when I was 10.

I still draw on random bits of paper.

I OFTEN LIE ON THE FLOOR, DOODLING ON ANY PIECE OF PAPER I CAN FIND WITH ANY PEN OR PENCIL I CAN GRAB.

THERE IS NO RIGHT OR WRONG WAY TO DRAW.

EXPERIMENTING WITH PAPER AND PENCILS HELPS YOU DECIDE WHAT YOU LIKE.

Using dotty lines or scribbly lines creates a different mood.

Cross-hatching or soft blending.

LIONARDO

HOLDING YOUR PENCIL IN DIFFERENT WAYS ALSO HELPS CREATE THESE DIFFERENT EFFECTS.

SKETCHBOOKS

If you love drawing, you may like to keep a sketchbook.

I have many sketchbooks, with different types of paper and in all sorts of sizes, which I use for various projects.

I'm on a roll with this drawing.

LEONARDO DA VINCI HAS THE MOST FAMOUS SKETCHBOOKS IN HISTORY, WITH OVER 7000 PAGES OF HIS AMAZING IDEAS, INVENTIONS AND DRAWINGS.

Try different types of sketchbooks to see what **you** like.

SOMETIMES I FEEL LIKE MY BRAIN WILL EXPLODE FROM TOO MANY IDEAS, SO I PUT THEM INTO MY SKETCHBOOKS.

T. AKAHĒ-REX

HERE'S WHAT I USE MY SKETCHBOOKS FOR:

I never know when I'll be inspired to draw, so I have a sketchbook tied to my belt, wherever I go.

Ideas for characters.

Writing stories. This is pretty messy, huh? I call it a **brain vomit** when I'm writing a book.

Drawings I've copied from other artists.

Things I see when I travel.

Reference drawings, or printouts and magazine clippings.

Faces

Sometimes Māui gets a
bit bored and frustrated.
From *How Māui Slowed the Sun*.

AS A STORYTELLER,
I WANT MY DRAWINGS TO
CONVEY THE CHARACTERS'
EMOTIONS.

HERE ARE SOME EXAMPLES
FROM MY BOOKS.

Claude D'Bonair looks
terrified as he is about to
leap from his crashing plane.
From *Flying Furballs 4 Most Wanted*.

Mary is gobsmacked when her lamb follows her to school.
From *Little Bo Peep and More*.

The famous composer Mozart looks like he has a secret to share with us.
From *Mozart, The Man Behind The Music*.

IMAGINE HOW BORING THESE PICTURES WOULD BE IF THEY DIDN'T HAVE EMOTIONS.

Are these boys working hard or hardly working?
From *Much Ado About Shakespeare*.

Mama cat looks rather cross with her pleading kittens.
From *Pussycat Pussycat and More*.

MOST ILLUSTRATORS WILL KEEP AN EXPRESSION SHEET CLOSE AT HAND WHEN THEY'RE DRAWING A CHARACTER.

HERE ARE SOME OF THE EXPRESSION SHEETS THAT I USED WHEN MAKING MY BOOKS.

Māui for *How Māui Fished Up The North Island*.

MR TIDDLES

SYD FISHUS

CLAUDE D'BONAIR

How do you feel?

With my hands.

Characters for *Flying Furballs*.

WHETHER YOU'RE DRAWING STICK FIGURES, CARTOONS, OR REALISTIC CHARACTERS, A SHEET OF EXPRESSIONS IS A USEFUL REFERENCE.

MOODY WILLIAM

William Shakespeare for *Much Ado About Shakespeare.*

Jimmy Grimholt for *Monkey Boy.*

I COULDN'T DRAW LIKE THIS WHEN I WAS YOUNG, SO LET'S TURN THE PAGE AND START WITH SOMETHING EVERYONE CAN DO.

DRAWING EXPRESSIONS
IS SUPER EASY.
ANYONE CAN DO IT!

THE TWO MOST
EXPRESSIVE ITEMS ON A FACE
ARE THE EYEBROWS AND MOUTH.
DRAW A CIRCLE FACE WITH TWO
SIMPLE DOTS FOR EYES.

why the long face?

Hmmm ...
that's a bit
boring isn't it?

Draw another face and try
it with a smiley mouth and
eyebrows that go up.

HAPPY

How do those down
eyebrows look with
a sad mouth?

MISCHIEVOUS

Use that smiley
mouth and make the
eyebrows go down.

GRUMPY

SAD

What about a
downward mouth with
eyebrows that go up?

NOW we have four basic emotions
just by moving the eyebrows and mouth up and down.

But what happens if we draw one eyebrow up and the other eyebrow down?

How about if we keep those eyebrows and just change the mouth?

CURIOUS

WITH TINY CHANGES WE CAN MAKE MORE COMPLEX EMOTIONS.

WONDERING

The eyes are the window to the soul.

LEONARDO KNOWS WHAT HE'S TALKING ABOUT. THE FACE CAN REVEAL WHAT THE CHARACTERS ARE FEELING ON THE INSIDE.

The mysterious expression on Leonardo's 'Mona Lisa' has been talked about for centuries.

THAT WAS PRETTY EASY, HUH?

LET'S TURN THE PAGE AND HAVE SOME FUN WITH IT...

Draw some funny shapes for faces

Now try and make different expressions by changing only the mouth and eyebrows.

If you get stuck, just draw the same eyes over and over and change the mouth ... then try it again with different eyes.

SHY

SCHEMING

IMPATIENT

FED UP

KNOWING

CONFUSED

SCEPTICAL

YOU CAN USE THESE SIMPLE EXPRESSIONS ON STICK FIGURES OR ...

EMBARRASSED

SURPRISED

Fill up your page and make a big beautiful mess.

SHOCKED

... ON MORE COMPLEX CHARACTERS.

TRY YOUR OWN FUNNY FACES, OR COPY MY DRAWINGS.

Every change creates a slightly different emotion. Think of some imaginative words to describe each expression.

HOW I DRAW A MAUISAURUS

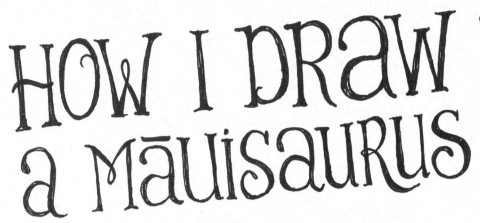

1
Start with basic ovals for the head and eyes.

2

3
Now draw a bigger oval below, for the body.

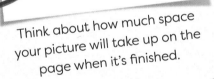

Think about how much space your picture will take up on the page when it's finished.

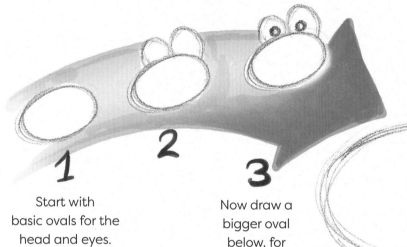

4 Join the head onto the body with long, flowing, snakey lines.

5
Add a swishy tail to the body.

These dinosaurs are from some of my books.

What do you call a dinosaur who's chasing you?

Do-you-think-he-saurus!

6 Add four flippers with simple triangle shapes.

Now it's time for some detail.

7

Some bubbles place your Māuisaurus underwater.

Add some of those expressions we've already learned.

How about some fish made of simple shapes like ovals, triangles and circles?

The fun part with dinosaurs is colouring them in. No one knows exactly what they looked like, so you can let your imagination go wild.

25

CREATING CHARACTERS

I've created lots of characters for many books and I've also worked as a character designer for animated TV shows. The most scary thing is looking at a blank piece of paper.

I CAN'T THINK WHAT TO DRAW.

I USUALLY BEGIN BY LIGHTLY DRAWING SOME SHAPES. FRUIT AND VEGETABLES HAVE INTERESTING SHAPES.

I've drawn a banana, a pear and a mushroom.

There are many other interesting shapes, like a strawberry, a carrot or a pineapple. What can you think of?

NOW I HAVE SOMETHING ON THE PAGE TO SPARK MY IMAGINATION.

Use your imagination to turn those shapes into characters.
Here's some doodles I've come up with …

Banana

I've added
ears, a face
and a tail.

This mushroom
could become a
kilt-wearing punk
with a robot arm.

This pear shape could be turned into a goofy
alien by adding legs, eyes and tentacles.

**SOME OF THE MOST RECOGNIZABLE
CHARACTERS ARE MADE OUT OF SIMPLE SHAPES.**

FRUITY CHARACTERS

When I create characters, I do lots of drawings.
I try many different options … maybe giving it long legs or short legs.
What about a big nose or a pointy nose, small eyes or big eyes?
I keep drawing and drawing until I see something I like.

Try turning the shape around.

Banana

TURN OFF YOUR BRAIN AND JUST DOODLE.

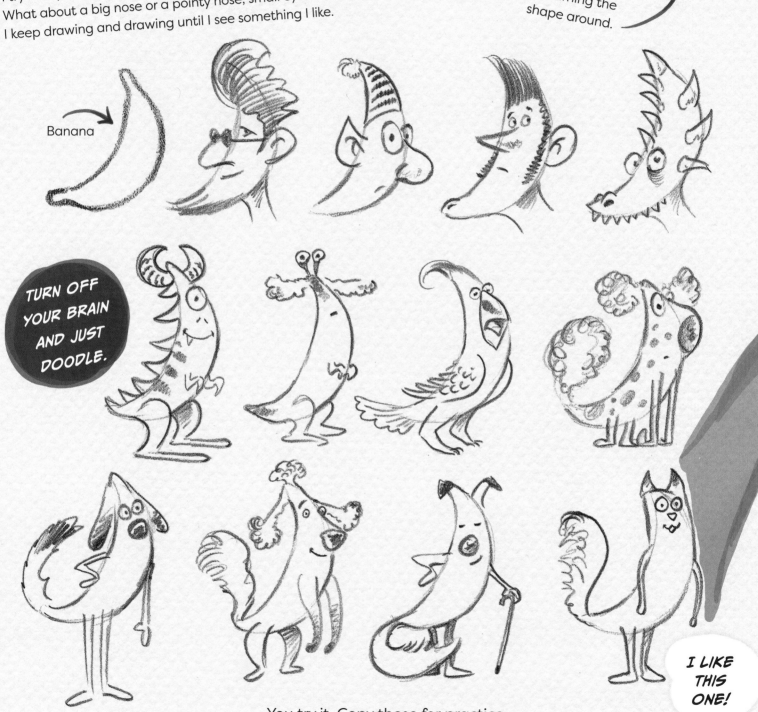

I LIKE THIS ONE!

You try it. Copy these for practice,
or make up your own characters based on fruity shapes.

DETAILS

Let's take our basic character and add details ...
clothing, a hat, bag, purse, jewellery, shoes.
Do they have long hair or short hair?
What kind of hairstyle do they have?

WITH DIFFERENT DETAILS YOUR BASIC CHARACTER COULD BE TRANSFORMED FROM THIS ...

Diamond tiara

Pearl necklace

Beauty spot

Big earrings

What are Kitty's hobbies?

Black gloves

GHOSTHUNTING

KITTY'S GUIDE TO

Purse

Floral pattern

Ribbons

Draw your sword.

CHARACTER DETAILS

Every little detail you add to a character gives them personality.

In *How Māui Fished Up the North Island*, I drew each of Māui's brothers a distinctive shape and size to make them easily recognisable.

Unique hair and decorations.

Designs for Claude's military uniform.

CLAUDE D'BONAIR
FLYING FURBALLS

Creating a character is like choosing an actor for a movie ... can they be brave, can they be scared, can they do kung fu?

I do a lot of research on costumes for my books, like these outfits worn hundreds of years ago in the time of Mozart or Shakespeare.

CLOTHING CAN SAY A LOT ABOUT A CHARACTER.

A striped shirt makes this character stand out, even in a crowd.

This character, from *The Weather Machine*, wears a onesie to match his childlike nature.

THERE CAN BE AN ENTIRE STORY IN EACH LITTLE DETAIL, LIKE THESE CHARACTERS FROM MONKEY BOY.

Will Williams got his tattoos in the South Pacific while working on a whaling ship.

A gruesome story lies behind Will's missing toes.

This is called a 'turn around'. I want to know what my character looks like from all sides.

MONKEY BOY

Mr Poe was struck by lightning and has a scar from shoulder to ankle.

EXERCISES FOR YOUR IMAGINATION

If you want a drawing challenge, take inspiration from one of the greatest artists of all time — Leonardo da Vinci.

You can find lots of ideas in the clouds, or marks on a wall.

You can be like Leonardo and stir your imagination, while at the same time exercising your drawing muscles (your brain and physical drawing skills need exercise, just like the body of an athlete does).

To start, take a piece of paper.
Get someone else to draw a scribble with a bright marker.
It's even more fun if they close their eyes.

Now begins the creative part.
Take your pencil and try to turn
that scribble into a drawing.

Our riches are the ideas in our heads, and they can never be taken from us.

WHAT COULD IT BE?

LET'S LOOK ON THE NEXT PAGE ...

Do you like my paw-trait?

35

Perhaps it could be the outline of a crazy beast.

SOME IDEAS WORK BETTER THAN OTHERS – THAT'S ALL PART OF THE FUN.

You will really exercise your imagination trying to create a drawing that incorporates the squiggle. The more you do, the more your creative muscle will grow.

NOW YOU TRY IT
If you have toddler in your family, you can even get them to draw a scribble for you.

In the end, you'll have a picture that you created together!

EVERYDAY INSPIRATION

LOOK AROUND YOUR HOME FOR INTERESTING SHAPES, LIKE THIS HAIR DRYER ... USE YOUR IMAGINATION TO TURN THEM INTO FANTASTICAL DRAWINGS.

HAIR DRYER

A HIGH-HEELED SHOE MIGHT MAKE AN INTERESTING SPACESHIP ...

COW 1

Off to explore the moo-niverse.

Some of the most famous designs are inspired by everyday things. The *Millennium Falcon* is based on a hamburger bun with an olive on the side, and a Star Destroyer looks just like a slice of pizza!

This drawing has really gone to pot.

With a bit of imagination, this saucepan ...

... could make a gnarly hot-rod tank!

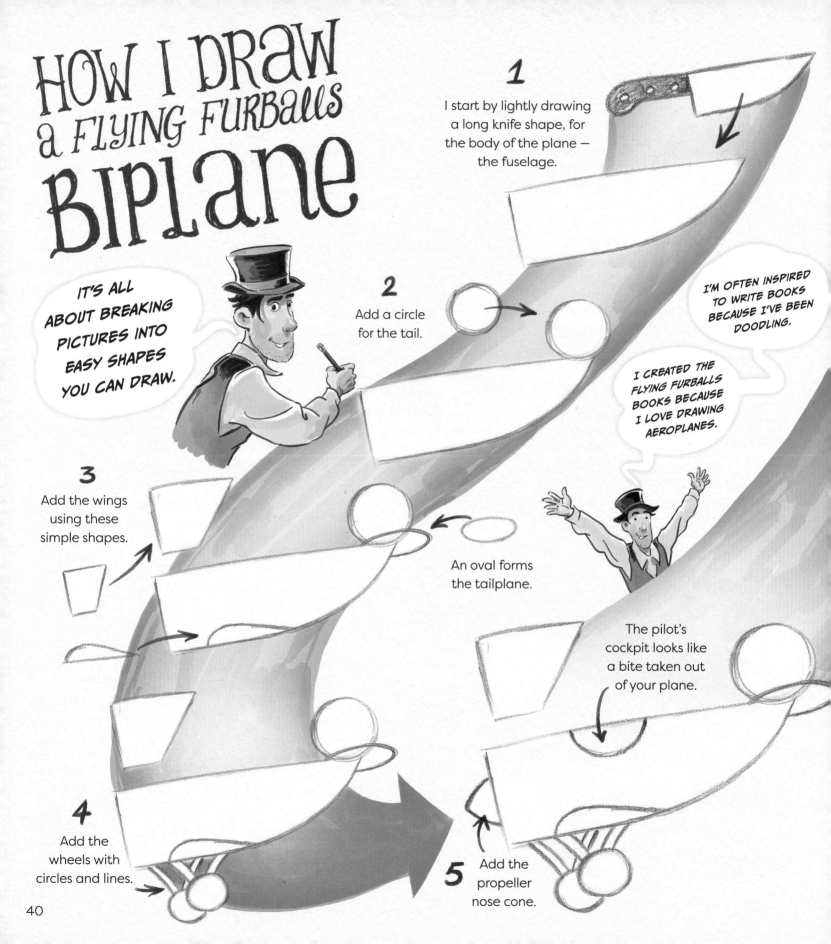

HOW I DRAW a FLYING FURBALLS BIPLANE

1
I start by lightly drawing a long knife shape, for the body of the plane — the fuselage.

IT'S ALL ABOUT BREAKING PICTURES INTO EASY SHAPES YOU CAN DRAW.

2
Add a circle for the tail.

I'M OFTEN INSPIRED TO WRITE BOOKS BECAUSE I'VE BEEN DOODLING.

I CREATED THE FLYING FURBALLS BOOKS BECAUSE I LOVE DRAWING AEROPLANES.

3
Add the wings using these simple shapes.

An oval forms the tailplane.

The pilot's cockpit looks like a bite taken out of your plane.

4
Add the wheels with circles and lines.

5
Add the propeller nose cone.

40

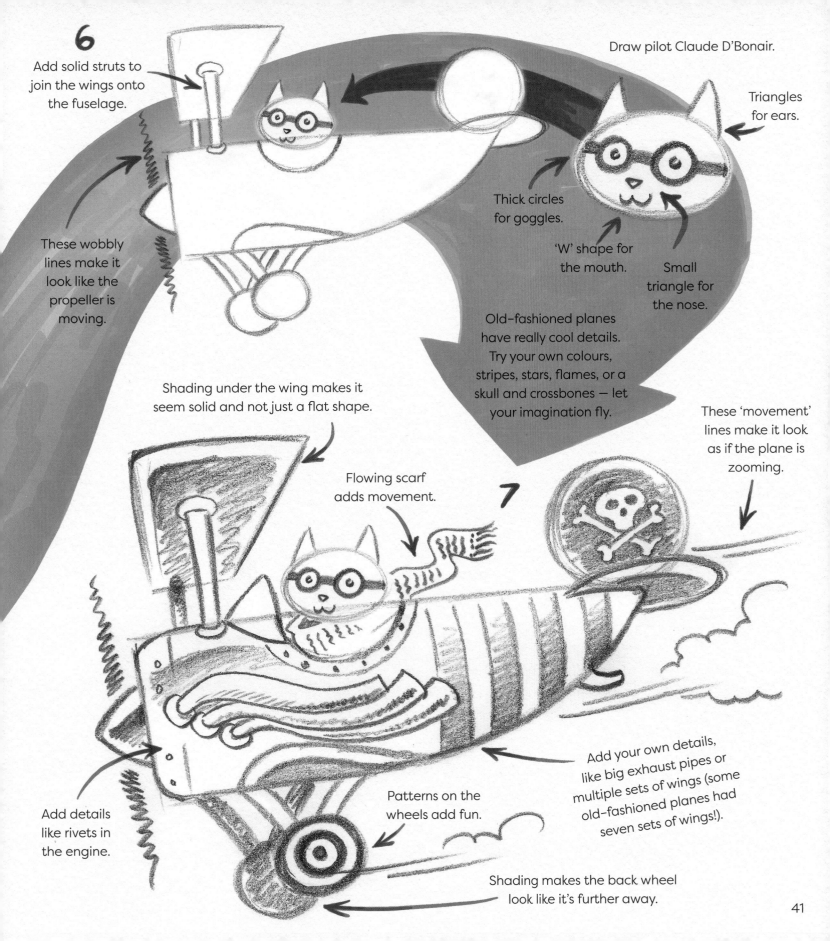

6

Add solid struts to join the wings onto the fuselage.

Draw pilot Claude D'Bonair.

These wobbly lines make it look like the propeller is moving.

Triangles for ears.

Thick circles for goggles.

'W' shape for the mouth.

Small triangle for the nose.

Old-fashioned planes have really cool details. Try your own colours, stripes, stars, flames, or a skull and crossbones — let your imagination fly.

Shading under the wing makes it seem solid and not just a flat shape.

Flowing scarf adds movement.

These 'movement' lines make it look as if the plane is zooming.

7

Add details like rivets in the engine.

Patterns on the wheels add fun.

Add your own details, like big exhaust pipes or multiple sets of wings (some old-fashioned planes had seven sets of wings!).

Shading makes the back wheel look like it's further away.

INSPIRATION FROM ARTISTS

My first book.

When I was seven, my mum read my brother and I *The Lord of the Rings*.

I loved drawing scenes of monsters and battles from the book.

I was inspired to write my own book to go with my pictures. I was copying many of the characters and ideas from *The Lord of the Rings*.

EACH ARTIST HAS THEIR OWN UNIQUE WAY OF DRAWING ... THEIR SIGNATURE STYLE. ALL THE GREAT ARTISTS LEARNED BY COPYING OTHER ARTISTS.

CHECK OUT EDGAR DEGAS ... ONE OF MY FAVOURITE ARTISTS.

Here's a painting I copied when I was about 10.

I drew these cartoons when I was 13, inspired by Murray Ball's *Footrot Flats*.

I still copy drawings by famous artists into my sketchbooks — and I'm still learning new skills.

Here's some of the books and artists who inspired me.

FOOTROT FLATS

THE LORD OF THE RINGS

DAVE MCKEAN

MORDILLO

LEONARDO DA VINCI

EDGAR DEGAS

JOHN HOWE

DR SEUSS

ASTERIX COMICS

BILL PEET

NORMAN ROCKWELL

All those ideas mix around inside your brain, and come out as your own style.

I discovered that I really like drawing historic scenes, and they feature in a lot of my illustrations.

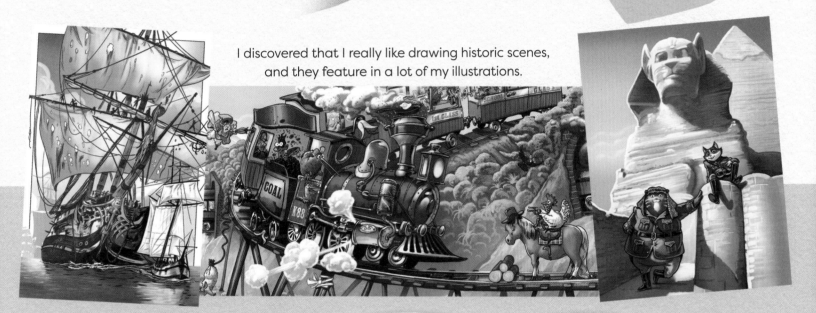

To develop my skills, I copied every painting in the Louvre Gallery in Paris ... twice!

The paintings I did after that looked like no one else's.

Copying your favourite artists is a great way to learn. That's what I did when I was young.

43

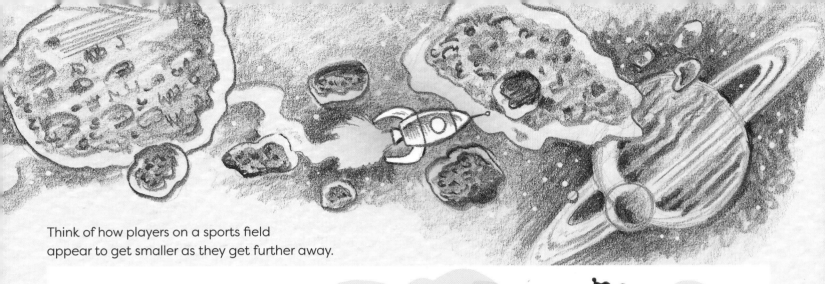

Think of how players on a sports field appear to get smaller as they get further away.

This player is bigger than the other lambs because it is closer.

These red lines help show how perspective works.

I'm Filippo Brunelleschi.*
I invented the technique of drawing perspective in Italy 600 years ago.

*Pronounced 'Brew-nel-es-key'.

The lampposts and narrowing stairs give this picture depth.

Whether it's planets in space or a row of All Black lambs, drawing figures and objects in different sizes can create the illusion of distance and perspective.

The reflection of the sun on the sea looks like a road disappearing into the distance.

Even the cloud in the sky can point off to the horizon.

You can create the illusion of distance by repeating similar objects in different sizes, like this big palm tree on the beach and the little palms on the island.

This ice cream is much bigger than the Merman's cone, making it look like it's close to us.

Seagulls flying in front of the squid help make the squid appear far away.

The squid looks gigantic because it's behind the pirate ship.

PERSPECTIVE IS LIKE MAGIC. LOOK AT THE OBJECTS ON THIS PAGE. DIFFERENT SIZES MAKE THEM SEEM LIKE THEY ARE CLOSER OR FURTHER AWAY.

The pathway gets narrower as it gets further away.

These fence posts also get smaller, making them look as if they go into the distance.

47

PERSPECTIVE IS JUST ONE TOOL AND IT'S GOOD TO LEARN IT.

BUT IT'S NOT THE ONLY WAY OF DRAWING.

This kind of 'flat' drawing, without perspective, creates its own fun feel.

AN ARTIST USES DIFFERENT TECHNIQUES AND STYLES DEPENDING ON THE STORY THEY ARE TRYING TO TELL.

Here the squid and the ship are the same size as they were on the last page. But without the illusion of perspective they now seem much smaller.

In this picture, the pirate ship is just a toy.

Without perspective, objects like these fence posts are all the same size as each other.

ROUGHS

ILLUSTRATORS START OFF WITH ROUGH DRAWINGS. SOMETIMES THEY'RE CALLED THUMBNAILS BECAUSE THEY ARE SMALL.

A painting like this doesn't just pop out of my head fully finished.

These sketches are a quick way for me to work out where I want all the elements to be on the page with rough shapes.

WITH ROUGHS I'M TRYING TO GET THE FOGGY IMAGE FROM MY MIND ONTO PAPER

ACTUAL SIZE
Some of my thumbnails really are the size of a thumbnail!

It might take lots of roughs before I draw something I like.

50

When I'm out walking,
I draw rough stick figures of people I see.
I'll work them into proper drawings
when I get home.

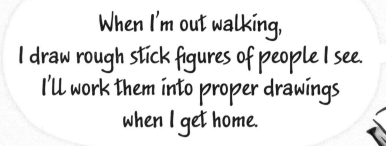

IF DRAWING STICK FIGURES IS
GOOD ENOUGH FOR LEONARDO,
IT'S GOOD ENOUGH FOR ME!

This way I can quickly draw figures in action,
like this character falling through the air.

At this stage I'm just
deciding where I want
the head, legs and arms.

I like this
pose.

Slowly I flesh
out the body of
my stick figure.

This is what it
looks like once
I've spent time
colouring it in.

I take time to add
in the details.

SHADING

SHADING IS A TRICK TO MAKE A SIMPLE OBJECT, LIKE THIS CIRCLE ...

LOOK AS IF IT HAS DIMENSION AND WEIGHT ... CRIKEY DINGO!

With shading we can make these basic flat shapes below look like a sphere, a cone and a cylinder.

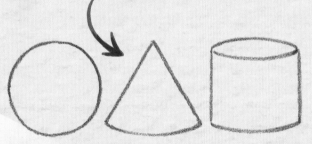

Try it yourself. Copy these shapes and try shading them in different ways ... with short pencil marks.

Let's imagine a torch is shining from this side. The shadows will appear away from the light, on the opposite side of the objects.

Straight lines ...   or curved lines.

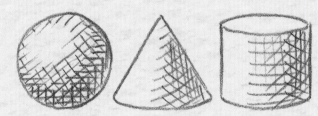

Cross-hatching.

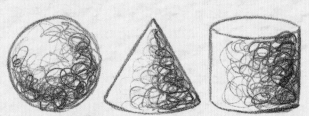

Scribbly lines.

How about blending soft and heavy pencil shading?

With practice you'll soon be able to add shading to more complex objects.

SOMETIMES I USE MY FINGER TO SMUDGE AND SOFTEN MY PENCIL MARKS. I BORROWED THAT IDEA FROM LEONARDO DA VINCI.

I call this kind of soft blending sfumato. It's Italian for smoky.

He looks like a shady character.

SHADOWS

SHADOWS ARE ANOTHER TOOL TO HELP ARTISTS TELL STORIES.

I use shadows in my illustrations to create all sorts of effects.

THESE DAPPLED SHADOWS HINT AT TREES, MAKING THE WORLD SEEM TO EXTEND BEYOND THE EDGES OF THE PICTURE.

Shadows can create atmosphere, like these long shadows at sunset.

Let's add a shadow to this drawing.

Look what happens when we move the shadow …

Now the pixie is flying!

THIS SHADOW MAKES THE PTEROSAUR SEEM HUGE, SOARING HIGH IN THE AIR.

EEEK!

Shadows can also add a sense of suspense ...

... or even show a looming figure that's off the page.

HOW I DRAW a UNICORN ...and more

1
I begin by lightly sketching basic ovals for the body and head.

2
These are only a rough indication of placement, NOT the final shape of the unicorn.

3
Join the body to the head with a curved neck.

4
Look, I've decided to move the head. That's the purpose of sketching.

I use swishing lines to form the tail.

Ears are small triangles.

I start adding details, like the horn.

These wavy lines make the mane look like it's flowing.

5
I try the legs in different positions, drawing them lightly with simple lines and circles for the joints.

Now I'm ready to start going over my sketchy lines to make them more solid.

6

TOP TIP
When drawing the joints in a horse's legs, I imagine them like a tennis ball in a sock.

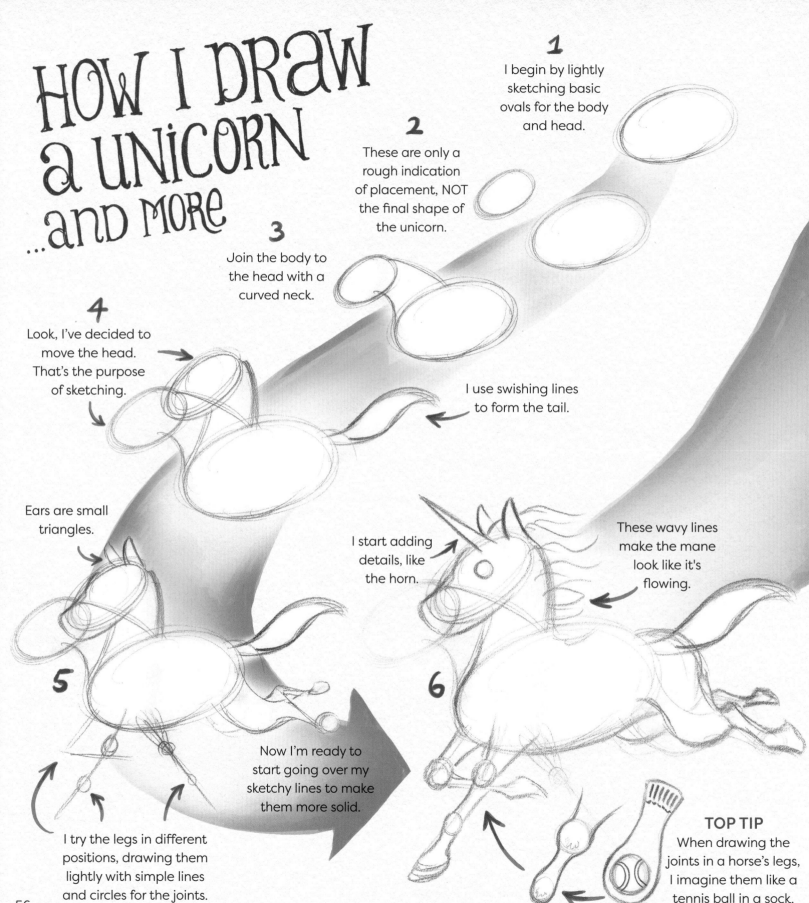

7

What's cooler than a unicorn?
A Pegasus unicorn!

I continue to add more details like nostrils and wings.

See how I've ignored this early option for a leg.

I start going over the shapes I like with heavier pencil marks — making little corrections as I go.

Little shadows make the feathers look overlapping.

TOP TIP
Wing feathers are long ovals overlapping like scales, with shorter feathers along the front edge of the wing.

What's cooler than a Pegasus unicorn?
A zebra Pegasus unicorn!

8

Shading under the jaw and wing help to give the image volume.

I thought zebra stripes would make it look even cooler.

Use finger blending to make the belly appear rounded.

Shade the legs on the far side.

Clouds and birds in the background make our zebra Pegasus unicorn stand out.

This shadow gives the feeling of soaring over the clouds.

COMPOSITION

WHEN I WAS YOUNG, I DIDN'T HAVE A CLUE WHAT THE WORD 'COMPOSITION' MEANT.

'COMPOSITION' IS JUST A FANCY NAME FOR WHERE YOU PLACE THINGS IN A DRAWING.

So how does composition change a picture?

In this basic example, think of three items on a page: the horizon line, the dinosaur and the sun.

Horizon line centred

What happens to our picture if we try those three items in different places on the page?

Horizon line down low

Moving the horizon line and other elements has a big effect on your drawing.

Horizon line up high

As well as where to place each item on the page, think about the shape of the image.

Long compositions like this are called 'landscape' pictures.

In these two pictures I've thought a lot about where I want to place each item, like the moon and the birds, or the plane and the Eiffel Tower.

Tall compositions are called 'portrait' pictures.

This is the title. I've left a big space in my picture where it will go.

WHAT ABOUT A SQUARE PICTURE, OR A ROUND PICTURE?

THERE'S NO RIGHT OR WRONG COMPOSITION. THE MAIN THING IS THAT YOU THOUGHT ABOUT IT!

COMPOSITION EXERCISE

HERE'S A FUN EXERCISE TO TRY.

Using simple stick figures, draw a picture of yourself standing next to a giant.

Most people will draw something like this ...

or maybe this ...

WHENEVER I DRAW A PICTURE, I IMAGINE THAT I'M MAKING A MOVIE ...

I PRETEND I HAVE A CAMERA THAT I CAN TAKE ANYWHERE IN MY IMAGINARY HELICOPTER

What would it look like close up?

What would it look like from up high?

HOW MANY DIFFERENT WAYS CAN YOU THINK OF PICTURING THIS SCENE?

What would it look like from down low?

I've been framed!

These compositions look at the picture from different angles.

From up high.

Imagine if the giant picked you up in its hand!

Extreme close-up.

SCARY.

Side on close-up.

Friendly.

MYSTERIOUS.

EACH COMPOSITION CAN HELP TELL DIFFERENT STORIES.

We can even show the giant without drawing it — remember those shadows?

From low down.

THE MORE YOU EXPERIMENT, THE BETTER YOU'LL GET.

YOU'LL SOON GET MORE CONFIDENT AT USING COMPOSITION IN YOUR ART.

TOP TIP
Sometimes I get my family to pose for a reference photo. Many artists use reference photos.

MAKING AN ILLUSTRATION

> WHEN I'M MAKING A BOOK, DRAWINGS ARE STEPPING STONES THAT HELP ME GET TO THE FINAL PICTURE.

I've got my expression sheet.

This illustration is going to be a landscape picture.

I've got my character designs.

> ONCE I HAVE A THUMBNAIL I LIKE, I'M READY TO DO A ROUGH DRAWING.

I try lots of different thumbnails.

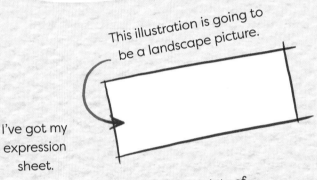

I've got my reference material.

THIS ROUGH SKETCH MIGHT TAKE ME A FEW MINUTES.

Next, I trace my sketch ... this time taking longer and adding details, fixing things, or leaving out parts I don't like.

HERE'S A SECRET ILLUSTRATOR TIP:

TRACE YOUR DRAWINGS.

A DRAWING LIKE THIS COULD TAKE SEVERAL HOURS.

I might have to trace my drawings many times before I'm ready for the final stage.

Even I trace my own work when I copy my drawings onto canvas.

Now I'm ready to make my final illustration. I trace over my drawing again and start colouring in.

THIS FINAL PAINTING COULD TAKE ME SEVERAL DAYS.

It's fun to experiment with different colouring techniques, like watercolour paints, pencils, or even digitally using a tablet.

Characters

Using your imagination

Shading

Perspective

Looking at other artists

Adding details

Expressions

Different mark making

Roughs and thumbnails

Sketchbooks

SO, NOW YOU'VE GOT A WHOLE LOT OF TRICKS, SKILLS AND IDEAS THAT YOU CAN USE TO DRAW SOMETHING REALLY **AWESOME.**

HERE'S WHAT MY HERO, MOZART, HAS TO SAY ...

Don't wait for permission to be artistic. If you feel it in your heart, JUST DO IT !

Come on, Mozart and Degas, let's get out of here.

Mon dieu!

WHOA, WAIT ... THAT'S NOT THE END, IS IT?

Sorry little guy, you've done your job. Time to say goodbye. Ka kite anō.